Caring for Your
Bird

Lynn Hamilton

Weigl Publishers Inc.

Project Coordinator
Diana Marshall

Design and Layout
Warren Clark
Katherine Phillips

Copy Editor
Jennifer Nault

Photo Research
Gayle Murdoff

Locate the bird prints throughout the book to find useful tips on caring for your pet.

Published by Weigl Publishers Inc.
350 5th Avenue, Suite 3304
New York, NY 10118-0069 USA
Web site: www.weigl.com

Library of Congress Cataloging-in-Publication Data available upon request from the publisher. Fax (507) 388-2746 for the attention of the Publishing Records Department.

ISBN 1-59036-067-2

Printed in the United States
3 4 5 6 7 8 9 0   06

Photograph and Text Credits
Every reasonable effort has been made to trace ownership and to obtain permission to reprint copyright material. The publishers would be pleased to have any errors or omissions brought to their attention so that they may be corrected in subsequent printings.

Cover: two birds perching (Henryk Kaiser/MaXx Images); **Behling and Johnson Photography:** pages 5, 6 middle, 10 bottom, 11 bottom, 13, 14, 18/19; **Comstock Images:** pages 3, 4, 9 bottom, 31; **Corel Corporation:** page 27; **Eric Ilasenko Photo/Digital:** title page, pages 6 right, 7 left, 8, 9 top, 11 top, 15 top, 16, 20 bottom, 23, 24, 25, 30; **MaXx Images:** page 10 top; **Ken Schwab/Photo Agora:** pages 6 left, 7 middle, 7 right; **Picturesof.net:** pages 12, 29; **Reneé Stockdale:** pages 15 bottom, 17, 20 top, 21, 22, 28; **©Warner Bros/Photofest:** page 26.

Moroney, Lynn. *Elinda Who Danced in the Sky*. San Francisco: Children's Book Press, 2001.

Contents

Feathery Friends

For centuries, people have enjoyed keeping birds as pets. They have admired the bird's grace and envied the bird's flying and singing abilities. Birds can be a variety of colors, shapes, and sizes. Birds can bring cheery sounds into your home with their whistling, chattering, singing, or talking. It is fun to watch them flutter and hop. Birds are intelligent and easy to train. They are usually indoor pets that do not require much space. A bird makes a good pet for someone who is allergic to furry animals.

▬ Birds make great companions. How many other pets can perch on your shoulder?

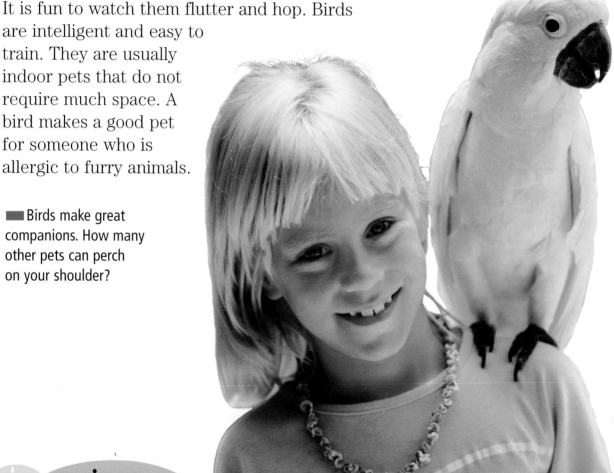

Fascinating Facts

- There are more than 9,000 **species** of birds in the world.
- In the United States, there are an estimated 11 million households containing pet budgies. About 2.6 million households own pet canaries.
- Animal organizations estimate that there are about 50 million pet birds in the United States.
- Two sets of vocal chords allow birds to sing two parts of a song at the same time.

There are many kinds of birds, each with special features and individual needs. Since a pet bird will be completely dependent on his owner for a healthy and comfortable home, it is important to be aware of his needs. A bird requires care and attention every day. In return for your efforts, you will have a happy and loving companion.

Birds pick their pals. They will let you know if they want to be petted, cuddled, or held.

◼ Learning about birds before bringing one home will help you meet all of your pet's needs.

Pet Profiles

There are many different **breeds** of birds. Birds come in a variety of colors, shapes, and sizes. Each type of bird has particular features and behaviors. Certain kinds of birds need constant attention and should not be left alone during the day. Others are more independent.

COCKATIELS

- Often gray, white, yellow, or light brown in color
- **Crests** on their heads are used to communicate with other birds
- Easily trained
- Whistle tunes and have some talking ability
- Adapt well to change
- Friendly; enjoy cuddling and handling
- Average life span of 6 to 15 years

CANARIES

- Often yellow, but can come in many colors
- Good natured, but prefer not to be handled
- Can be messy eaters
- Excellent singers, especially male canaries
- Independent; can be left alone
- Average life span of 7 to 10 years

BUDGIES

- Also called budgerigars
- Many colors, such as blue and green
- Adult male's **cere** is blue, while adult female's cere is brown or pink
- Very affectionate
- Can talk and learn well from children's voices
- Very friendly and talkative
- Average life span of 4 to 8 years

Parrots, and many other large birds, can be very demanding. They require a great deal of attention. Many large birds live to be 50 to 100 years old. Since finches and canaries are the least demanding types of birds, they have become popular pets. Knowing the features of each type of bird will help you to choose the best bird for your home.

LOVEBIRDS

- Green, with different colors on their head and tail
- Pairs huddle together, but despite their name, some may not get along
- Active and curious
- Require toys and time outside of the cage
- High-pitched chatter
- Very social; if alone often, should have a companion
- Average life span of 10 to 15 years

DOVES

- Often white, gray, or brown
- Can grow larger than a chicken
- Strong fliers
- Easily tamed
- Frequently make soft cooing sounds
- Require plenty of sunlight for warmth
- Do not enjoy handling
- Average life span of 6 to 11 years

CONURES

- All colors and sizes
- Active, playful; require large cages
- Enjoy toys but can often destroy them
- Very noisy; loud, screeching voices
- Affectionate, enjoy handling and cuddling
- Some types may not be suitable for children
- Can be expensive to buy
- Average life span of 10 to 25 years

Bird Beginnings

Birds may have gradually developed from reptiles. Scientists found the remains of a 147-million-year-old creature called *Archaeopteryx*. While it had the features of a reptile, it also had feathers. Other scientists believe that birds developed from dinosaurs that grew feathers.

Fossils of birds dating back 90 million years have been found in the United States. These fossils reveal similar features to present-day water birds, such as the loon. About 65 million years ago, relatives of modern birds, such as **perching** birds, first appeared. Over the centuries, birds developed stronger muscles and wings, and skeletons well suited to flying.

Caged birds cannot learn survival skills from other birds in the wild. It is important to prevent tame birds from flying free.

The scaly skin on birds' legs and their ability to lay hard-shelled eggs links birds to reptiles and dinosaurs.

■ Today, many clubs, shows, and competitions attract bird lovers around the world.

Birds were among the first animals to be **domesticated** by humans. The Chinese raised falcons around 2000 BC to catch pheasants and rabbits for the emperor's dinner. In 1500 BC, the queen of Egypt owned hawks. Later, Christopher Columbus took two parrots back to Europe as gifts for Queen Isabella of Spain.

Budgies first appeared in England in 1840. During World War II, soldiers brought canaries to battle. Soldiers sent canaries into tunnels behind enemy lines to detect bad air and poisonous gas. During the 1950s, budgies became popular pets in the United States.

■ Explorer Christopher Columbus found parrots in the New World in 1492.

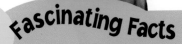

Fascinating Facts

- Miners used canaries to warn them of dangerous gases in the mines. If the canaries stopped singing or became unconscious, miners were alerted to danger.
- Many pigeons will return home even if they are released far away. During World War I, carrier pigeons helped British and American armies deliver important messages over long distances and between ships at sea.

Life Cycle

Some people raise their pet birds from eggs to adulthood. Others buy their birds from pet stores or bird breeders. It is important to know how a bird develops so you can properly care for your pet's needs at all stages of his life.

Eggs and Hatching

Adult birds sit on their eggs to keep them warm. The warmth helps the baby bird grow within the egg. Moving or touching an egg can harm the bird inside. Germs from your hands can pass through the shell. The chick will use his beak to break through the shell 2 to 5 weeks after he has been laid.

Maturity

Many birds reach adulthood within a few months to a year. Others take 2 or 3 years to become fully grown. Most birds molt once each year. During molting, birds shed their feathers and grow new ones. A molting bird can be made more comfortable with plenty of fresh water and many opportunities for baths. Try not to buy a bird during molting, as this is already a very stressful time for a bird. The life span of different pet bird varieties can range from 5 to 100 years.

Fascinating Facts

- Baby birds make sounds to communicate their needs. Their parents know which sounds mean they are hungry and which sounds mean they are scared.

Chicks

Some chicks have feathers and can move around and feed on their own right after hatching. Others are blind and featherless. By the end of the second week, most chicks are covered in soft feathers, called down, and have some wing feathers. They may be a little wobbly and sometimes may lose their balance. If a caged bird falls out of his nest, it is safe to gently put him back. When handling young birds, it is important to be extremely gentle.

Fledglings

A chick becomes a fledgling when he begins to develop flight feathers. Fledglings start to explore their surroundings, but they still rely on their parents for food. If humans interfere too much or handle the young, some birds will abandon their babies. At about 2 weeks out of the nest, most birds can provide for themselves.

Picking Your Pet

Knowing as much as you can about birds will help you be a responsible pet owner. As much as you want the perfect pet for yourself, it is important to be the right person for your pet. Consider the following questions to help guide your decision.

What Can I Afford?

Pet bird prices vary. Large birds or trained birds can be expensive. With any bird, you will have to buy a cage and cage cover; toys, such as mirrors and bells; and accessories, such as perches, stands, and swings. Bird food is an ongoing cost, and different birds require different foods. Medical and **veterinary** costs also add to the expense of owning a bird.

Even a beautiful song can seem too loud. Keep this in mind when choosing your bird to prevent disturbing family members.

■ Exotic birds, such as macaws and Amazon conures, are often very expensive.

Will a Bird Be Able to Rely on Me?

A bird's cage must be cleaned very regularly. Daily visits to entertain pet birds are important for these social animals. Vocal, social birds require a great deal of attention. They may pluck out their feathers or destroy items in their cage if they feel ignored. Training a pet bird also takes time and effort.

Is My Home Suitable?

Your house will require enough space for a bird cage. Your bird may need to fly around in your home for exercise, especially if her cage is small. Family members with allergies to feathers or who already own other pets should be considered. It is important to have a bird-friendly home.

Cats and birds do not always get along. If there is already a cat in the house, she may try to eat a new bird.

Fascinating Facts

- Most birds can be kept in a standard cage. An aviary is a larger enclosure in which several birds can fly around.
- While two birds can be good company for each other, not all birds get along.
- Both male and female canaries begin to sing as early as 4 weeks of age. Females rarely sing after about 6 months of age. Due to their singing abilities, male canaries are more costly than females.
- Parrots and other large birds can produce ear-piercing screams.

Bird Basics

Before bringing your new feathered friend home, it is a good idea to buy a few basic supplies. These will help you provide a safe and comfortable living space for your pet bird.

While the cage should be two or three times the width of the bird's **wingspan**, no cage can be too large. If you do not take your bird out for exercise, his cage should be much larger. Since most birds love to chew, no part of a cage or its contents should be toxic or breakable. A secure door will prevent escapes. Some birds may be afraid of the dark. Using a night-light or uncovering their cage can calm their fear of the dark.

When arranging the items in your bird's cage, do not place his food bowl where his droppings may fall.

The bars of a cage should be spaced so the bird's feet and head cannot get caught between them.

Fascinating Facts

• Many household items are a danger to birds. Toilet lids should always be shut to prevent small birds from drowning while trying to take a drink of water from the toilet bowl.

Inside the cage, perches of different sizes and positions help to keep a bird's feet healthy. While sandpaper perches can wear down overgrown claws, they can also hurt a bird's feet. Feeders allow food to drop into a tray as needed. Some birds drink from containers with steel spouts. Other birds prefer bowls.

Birds love to play, and toys, such as bells and ladders, encourage exercise. Since canaries enjoy swinging, cages with sharp corners that could harm them should be avoided. A variety of toys can help your bird stay healthy and active.

A small pet carrier can be your bird's temporary home for trips to the **veterinarian**, and when you clean his cage.

■ There is more involved in owning a bird than buying a bird and a cage.

■ Many birds, such as lovebirds, are very social and do not like to be left alone.

Eating Like a Bird

Different birds need and enjoy different combinations of foods. Seeds are a part of many bird diets. Since **softbills** cannot crack seeds they enjoy fruit instead. Live insect food is a healthy part of some bird diets. Birds also need vegetables, such as spinach. Food and fresh drinking water must be provided at least once a day.

Some human foods are not safe for birds. Salty snack foods, chocolate, and avocados are poisonous to birds.

Seed mixes that are suited to specific bird types are available at pet stores.

Birds need different amounts of food at various ages and times of their life. The more active the bird, the more food she needs. Most birds eat little meals throughout the day. Pet birds should never go for hours without food.

Cuttlefish bones are recommended for birds who eat mostly seeds. The bones provide birds with calcium. In addition, budgies need to pick at a block of iodine in their cage. This substance, which helps birds molt, is often lacking in a budgie's diet. Some experts recommend feeding birds grit to help their digestion. Grit is composed of small particles of sand and shells, so it must be used carefully. Your veterinarian is the best source for advice on proper feeding of your pet bird.

Your pet bird should always have access to fresh water.

Fascinating Facts

- When a bird is molting, diet supplements, such as extra vitamins, may be needed.
- A bird's body temperature is high. As a result, they need plenty of food for fuel. Some birds must eat up to one-third of their body weight in food each day.
- Birds can be picky eaters. This may be caused by stubbornness or illness. Owners should be aware of their pet bird's regular eating patterns, so they can detect sudden changes due to sickness.
- Some birds may vomit their seeds to feed other birds, their reflections in the mirror, or even their owners.

From Feathers to Feet

Birds are the only animals that are covered in feathers. A bird's skeleton is sturdy, but also very light. Birds have strong wing muscles. They also have air sacs that help them breathe faster than any other animal. A flying pigeon breathes 450 times per minute. A running human breathes 30 times per minute. These features enable birds to fly.

Contour feathers found on the tail, wings, and body give birds their shape. Flight feathers on the wings and tail help them fly. Beneath these feathers are down feathers, which keep birds warm.

A bird's tail controls direction when flying. It also helps control landings. For some birds, the tail is used to attract mates. Often, when a pet bird's tail bobs, it means he is ill.

Nine air sacs fill most of the space in a bird's body. The air sacs help move air throughout the bird's body. They allow the bird to breathe high in the sky, where there is less oxygen, and to maintain regular body temperature.

Many birds can turn their head 180 degrees.

Most birds have large eyes on the sides of their head. This allows them to see approaching danger from either direction. Each eye is protected by three eyelids.

Birds' beaks are made of bone and **keratin**. Some birds have hooked beaks that help them climb, and eat nuts and seeds. Birds also use their beaks to **preen** themselves. The beak continues to grow throughout a bird's life. A bird wears down his beak by rubbing it against objects.

A bird's two strong legs are protected by scales. Birds' legs help them leap into the air.

Some birds have two toes facing forward and two toes facing backward on each foot. These are useful for climbing. In the wild, claws help the birds capture **prey**. Birds use their clawed toes to help them grip their perch.

PARROT

Bird Bath

Most birds enjoy a bath to keep clean. All bird cages should have a sturdy bowl that is big enough for a bird to splash around in. Since many birds love to shower, a gentle mist from a spray bottle can be a pleasant way for your bird to bathe.

Birds' claws need to be trimmed. A small bird can be picked up by placing one hand over her back and holding her gently but firmly. Her neck will fit between your thumb and first finger. You may need a helper to handle a large bird. Claw trimming is quite tricky. Your veterinarian should trim your pet bird's claws the first few times. This will allow you to watch how it is done.

Your pet bird's bath water should be fresh, shallow, and lukewarm in temperature.

Fascinating Facts

- Clean, shiny feathers are a sign of good health. Healthy budgies should have unruffled feathers.
- Some veterinarians recommend wing trims for certain birds. Wing trims prevent birds from flying away and injuring themselves. Improper wing trims can cause serious injury. Only a veterinarian should perform the task.
- Baths encourage birds to preen. Using their beaks, birds use oil from a gland at the base of their tails. Preening is important because it removes dirt and **parasites**, and keeps feathers waterproof and healthy.

Bird cleanliness begins with the cage. The cleaner the cage, the cleaner the bird. Droppings at the bottom of the cage should be cleared away daily. At least once a week, the cage should be cleaned thoroughly. The cage should be **disinfected** every few months. Wash all dishes and replace the cage lining. When cleaning the cage, remember to wash your bird's toys as well. Mild soap may be used for daily cleaning. Since birds are very sensitive to strong smells, ask your veterinarian to recommend a safe disinfectant cleaner.

Birds can drown in a very small amount of water. Be careful not to fill their bath bowls too high.

Gloves or a small towel can protect you from nips and scratches when caring for your bird.

Healthy and Happy

Certain measures will help keep your bird healthy. Choosing a veterinarian that you trust and know well is a good start. At home, try to place your bird's cage far away from drafts, extreme heat, or direct sunlight. Since loud noises make birds nervous, always keep the cage far away from the television. The kitchen is not a good location for your bird's cage because cooking fumes and cleaning products can make him sick.

To prevent your bird from flying into windows or mirrors, be sure to cover them with curtains or decals.

Many veterinarians do not treat birds. A specialist in bird care is called an avian veterinarian.

Fascinating Facts

- Some birds sleep standing up. They have tendons in their legs that cause their toes to grip on to the perch.
- Birds can develop allergies, especially when new items or foods are introduced into their environment. Sneezing and feather-picking are signs of allergies.

Before releasing your bird from his cage, make sure the room is safe. Birds can fly into dangerous places, such as vents and ovens. Close all doors and windows. You should also remove foods, plants, and ornaments that may be poisonous or cause injury.

Check your bird's behavior and appearance often. Have his eating and sleeping habits, activity level, temper, or weight changed? Does he have runny eyes or tattered feathers? Are his droppings normal? A canary that stops singing is probably ill or molting. If your bird has worn-out feathers or does not molt, he may be ill. Your veterinarian can answer these questions, give your bird a checkup, and treat him if he is ill or hurt.

▬ Most birds benefit from free-flying time. It is good exercise and prevents boredom.

Bird Behavior

Give your bird plenty of time to get to know you before handling, taming, or training her. Placing the cage at eye level helps establish trust. Begin by gradually putting your hand into her cage. This should be done with caution, as some birds may bite. If your bird is startled, allow her to calm down before you try to handle her again. A hungry bird can often be encouraged to sit on your hand to take food from you. It is always a good idea to give your bird a treat whenever she has learned something new or progressed in her training.

Kissing your bird is not a good idea. Some birds bite, which may leave you with a bleeding lip.

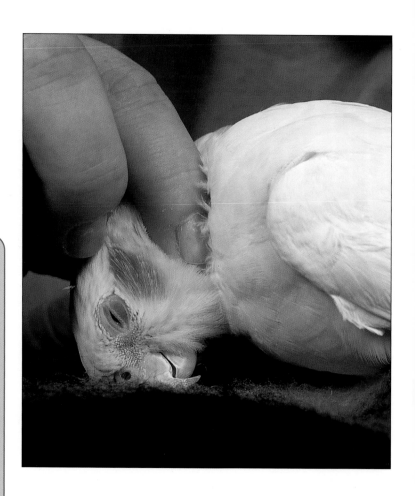

Many birds, such as cockatiels, love being petted and cuddled by their owners.

Pet Peeves

Birds do not like:
- cats treating them like prey
- shouting or loud noises
- owners squirting them with water instead of gently misting
- surprise or rapid approaches from outside their field of vision
- owners staring directly into their eyes while approaching

Teaching birds to talk calls for plenty of patience. It is helpful to remove all distractions, including other birds or humans. Having one teacher works best, as it is less confusing for your bird. Begin with one or two simple words, such as "Hi, birdie." Be prepared to repeat the words often. Say them every time you pass your bird's cage. The more words your bird learns, the easier it will be for him to speak. Since birds enjoy socializing, learning this way is fun for them.

▆▆▆ Talking to your pet bird often will encourage him to talk back.

Fascinating Facts

- Mynas and parrots are among the best bird talkers. Mynas have been known to copy barking dogs and flushing toilets. One parrot from England could say nearly 800 words.
- The part of the brain that controls learning is bigger in parrots than in many other birds. As a result, parrots can learn tricks.
- The earlier birds start to learn to talk, the better talkers they become.

Above and Beyond

Humans have admired and appreciated birds throughout history. They saw birds gracefully soaring through the sky and dreamed of having the same freedom. Inventors modeled airplane wings after birds' wings.

Birds appear as **symbols** in stories and legends. For instance, the dove has come to represent peace. Many stories tell of a dove that is released and returns with an olive branch. This meant that a war was over or suffering had ended. Ancient legends explained that witches could turn into any bird except the dove.

From Tweety to Big Bird, feathery friends are featured in many movies, books, and folk tales around the world.

▬ Tweety, the little yellow canary, first appeared on television in 1942.

Fascinating Facts

- The national symbol of the United States is the bald eagle.
- President Thomas Jefferson had a pet mockingbird, named Dick, at the White House. The president would let his faithful companion sit on his shoulder wherever he went.

A Feathery Fable

"Elinda Who Danced in the Sky" is a folk tale from Estonia. Generations of children have listened to the story of the sky goddess named Elinda who guides the **migration** of birds. The beautiful princess is born from a tiny bird's egg. As she grows up, she begins to direct the birds in their migration. One day, Elinda falls in love with Prince Borealis, the lord over the dancing lights of the sky. She begins to weave a wedding veil of stars. When she finds out that the prince will not return to her, Elinda's heart breaks. In her sorrow, she forgets her important duty to the birds. Many birds are lost. To help Elinda overcome her sorrow, some birds carry her up to the sky, where she is crowned with stars. From this day forward, whenever the night sky is clear, her wedding veil can be seen. This is how the birds helped create the Milky Way.

From Lynn Moroney's *Elinda Who Danced in the Sky*.

Pet Puzzlers

How much do you know about feathers and flying? If you can answer the following questions correctly, you may be ready to own a pet bird.

Q Why do pet birds need toys and accessories?

Since pet birds still have many of the needs and instincts of their relatives in the wild, they can easily become bored and restless in a cage. Toys and accessories keep birds active, energetic, healthy, and playful.

Q How often should pet birds be fed?

While this may vary depending on the type and size of a particular pet bird, most veterinarians agree that there should always be food in your pet bird's bowl. This allows her to feed whenever she is hungry.

Q Why do birds molt?

Since feathers cannot repair themselves, birds shed worn-out or broken feathers, allowing new, healthy feathers to grow in. Molting occurs at least once each year.

Q What does it mean if a pet bird plucks her feathers?

Feather plucking is usually a means to communicate unhappiness or illness. If your pet bird is ill or feeling lonely, she may pluck out her feathers to let you know.

Q How do birds sleep standing up?

Special tendons in birds' legs cause their toes to grip branches, perches, or swings. This allows a bird to sleep standing up.

Q What role did canaries play in World War II?

Soldiers sent canaries into tunnels behind enemy lines to detect bad air or poisonous gases.

Bird Calls

Before you buy your pet bird, write down bird names that you like. Some names may work better for a female bird. Others may suit a male bird. Here are just a few suggestions:

Ginger

Daisy

Paulie

Peeps

Glider

Dolly

Buddy

Piper

Howie

Tweety

Frequently Asked Questions

Does my bird need extra vitamins?

A well-balanced diet usually means that additional vitamins and minerals are not necessary. There can be exceptions, such as when a bird is molting or sick. It is always best to ask for your veterinarian's advice before giving your pet bird extra vitamins or any medications.

How often should my bird's beak and claws be trimmed?

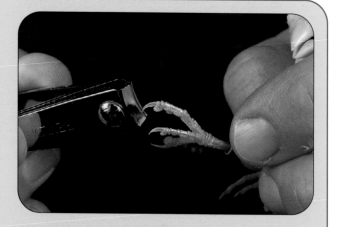

If your bird does not keep his beak trimmed by chewing, he will need occasional trimming by a veterinarian. Birds' nails are often kept at the proper length through their daily activities. If nails begin to interfere with perching or are getting caught in the cage bars, it is time for a trim. In all cases, your veterinarian can trim your bird and may even show you how to trim his claws.

Is it normal for my bird to pull out her feathers?

Ruffled feathers and feathers on the bottom of the cage are a normal part of molting. If your bird is pulling out her feathers, there may be a behavior problem or physical problem. For any long-lasting, unusual behavior, it is best to ask your veterinarian for advice.

More Information

Animal Organizations

You can help birds stay healthy and happy by learning more about them. Many organizations are dedicated to teaching people how to care for and protect their pet pals. For more bird information, write to the following organizations:

The Association of Avian Veterinarians
P.O. Box 811720
Boca Raton, FL 33481

American Federation of Aviculture
P.O. Box 7312
N. Kansas City, MO 64116

Web Sites

To answer more of your bird questions, go online and surf to the following Web sites:

Care for Animals
www.avma.org/careforanimals/
animatedjourneys/animatedfl.asp

American Humane Association
www.americanhumane.org/kids/default.htm

Pet Place
www.petplace.com

Words to Know

breeds: groups of animals that share specific characteristics

cere: waxy piece of skin above the beaks of some birds

crests: tufts of feathers on a bird's head

cuttlefish bones: bones from cuttlefish, a ten-armed sea creature

disinfected: cleaned to destroy germs

domesticated: tamed and made to live among people

fossils: remains of animals and plants from long ago found in rocks

keratin: the same strong substance found in human fingernails

migration: seasonal movement of a group of animals from one region to another

parasites: organisms that live on or in other organisms to obtain nutrients

perching: type of bird that roosts, or rests, on an elevated pole or rod, which is called a perch

preen: using the beak to groom by arranging and cleaning feathers

prey: animals that are hunted and eaten by other animals

softbills: birds that eat mainly soft food, such as fruit

species: a group of organisms that shares biological features

symbols: things used to stand in for and represent things, feelings, and ideas

veterinarian: animal doctor

veterinary: medical treatment of animals

wingspan: distance between the two wingtips of a bird when flying

Index